Selling on 'The River'

The eBay Seller's Guide to Amazon.com

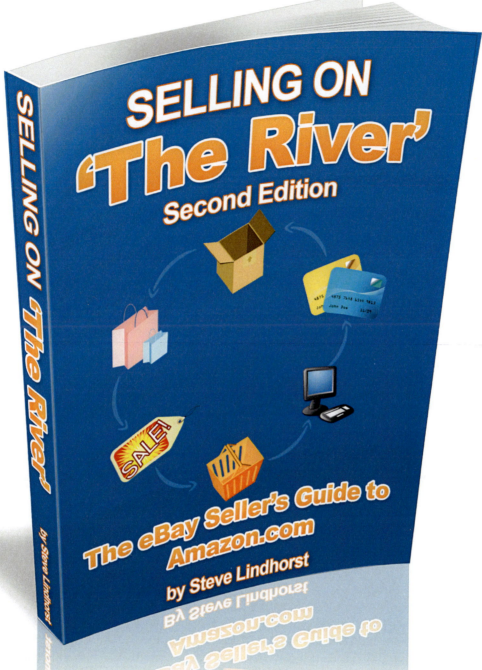

The first-ever guide to Amazon.com designed especially for eBay Sellers

by former eBay University Instructor Steve Lindhorst

Foreword by Skip McGrath

Copyright © 2008-2009 GenuineSeller.com

ISBN 978-1442191839

EAN-13 9781442191839

www.SellingOnTheRiver.com

All rights reserved.

No part of this book may be reproduced or transmitted in any form or by any means, electronic, mechanical, photocopying, recording, or otherwise, without the prior written permission of the publisher.

Legal Disclaimer

This book contains statements and claims relating to how much money one can make using these methods. Please understand that these are estimates and projections. The exact amount you can make will depend on your talent, your experience and how hard you work at it.

All websites and URLs in this book are current at the time of publication. However, websites change, may be taken down or moved. The publisher and the author are not responsible for the content contained in any website mentioned or featured in this book, nor shall they be liable for any loss or damage arising from the information contained in this book. As with anything you do in life there is no substitute for good judgment.

Table of Contents

TABLE OF CONTENTS 3

FOREWORD BY AUTHOR AND EBAY GOLD POWERSELLER, ... 7

INTRODUCTION 9

WHAT TO EXPECT FROM THIS BOOK 12

CUTTING THROUGH A JUNGLE OF CONFUSION 13

CAN I MAKE MONEY AT THIS? 14
    Where Will I Get Things to Sell? 15
    How Do I Know What People Want to Buy? 15
    How Do I Set Prices For My Items? 16
    How Do I Ship the Things I Sell? 16
    Is the Amazon community as safe as eBay's community? 17

BENEFITS OF MULTI-CHANNEL SELLING 18
    Do you have your eggs in one basket? 18
    A Larger – and Different Audience 18

WHY AMAZON? 20
    What about 'eBay alternative' sites?" 20
    Another Basket for Your Eggs 20

USING WHAT YOU'VE LEARNED ON EBAY 21
    Product Sourcing 21

YOUR AMAZON SELLER ACCOUNT 23
    The Amazon Marketplace and Seller Central 23
    Which is best for you? 24
    Registering as an Amazon Seller 24
    Seller Fees 26
    The Product Detail Page – a Fundamental Difference 27

AMAZON SELLER ACCOUNT LEVELS 28
    Individual Seller 28
    Amazon Pro Merchant Subscription 28
    Amazon Merchants 29

CATEGORY RESTRICTIONS 30

How Do I Get Approved to Sell in a Restricted Category?...31
The Pre-order Report...32

CLASSIFYING YOUR PRODUCT 33
The Universal Product Code (UPC) 33
I Create One-of-a-Kind Items, with No UPC, Can I Sell on Amazon? 34
How to Get a UPC Code for Your Products 34
How Do I Request an UPC Exemption? 37

CREATING A PRODUCT DETAIL PAGE 38
Four Steps to Creating a *New* Product Detail Page 38
STEP 1: Classify Your Product 39
STEP 2: Identify Your Product 40
STEP 3: Add the Details 42
STEP 4: Sell 46
The Condition Note Attribute – Learn it, love it. 47
Condition Notes Best Practices 49
Things to Avoid in Your Condition Notes 50

PRICING STRATEGIES & SHIPPING OPTIONS 51
Amazon Sales Rank 52
Autopricers / Undercutting / Price Cutters 53
Set Your Price 53

SHIPPING ON AMAZON 54
Video: Creating a Product Detail Page 56
Me too" listings..57
Video: Creating a "Me Too" Listing 56

MANAGING YOUR INVENTORY 58
ASIN (Amazon Standard Identification Number) 58
SKUs and Your Growing Inventory 59
Fulfillment by Amazon (FBA) 59
Vacation Settings 60

MAKING THE SALE AND GETTING PAID 62
Amazon Payments 62
Chargebacks 63

PACKING AND SHIPPING YOUR ITEMS 64
Packing Best Practices 64
How to Print Shipping Labels for Amazon Orders with PayPal 65

  PayPal MultiOrder Shipping 66
  Customer Service 66

DEALING WITH AMAZON – POLICIES YOU SHOULD KNOW 67
  Amazon's A-to-z Guarantee 67
  New Seller Reviews 68
  Velocity Limits 69
  Feedback (yes, they have it here too) 70
  Amazon Phone Support 71

SUMMARY 72

RESOURCES FOR AMAZON SELLERS 73

Foreword by author and eBay Gold PowerSeller, Skip McGrath

When I started selling on eBay in 1999 it was a place where virtually any little guy or gal could sell almost anything and make scads of money. You can still make good money today, but eBay, like everything else, has changed and grown over time. Today eBay is more complex and more competitive. One of the big changes over the past few years is that fixed price listings now account for a large portion of eBay sales. There are still plenty of buyers who like the excitement of the auction format, but more and more people prefer to make an immediate purchase. Amazon.com tried the auction format for a while, but it never really got traction as eBay was so dominant. But Amazon has grown to become the number one fixed-price buying site on the internet and as such has attracted many of the same sellers who also sell on eBay, including myself.

I have been selling on Amazon for the past two years with mixed results. When Steve asked me to review his book I was delighted. I knew that although I was highly skilled on eBay, I didn't really understand how to take full advantage of the Amazon platform. What an eye opener. I wasn't even half way through the book when I went into my Amazon account and started making changes. It was unbelievable how many simple things I was doing wrong. Since getting Steve's book, I have been spending about 30 minutes a day, just going through my listings and tuning them up.

You can tell by the way he writes that Steve is a great teacher. He patiently takes you through all of the steps to set up your account correctly, list and sell your items and how to optimize your listings to increase sales. The other eye opener is that is was so easy once you had someone to show you the way. Best of all Steve showed me how I can use all of the knowledge I have acquired on eBay and apply it to Amazon.

No, I am not leaving eBay, but now that I have a map and a plan, I will be devoting more of my time and resources to Amazon.

Skip McGrath

www.skipmcgrath.com

Introduction

In the Spring of 2008 I released the first edition of "Selling on 'the River'" and I was astounded, and very gratified at the response. Since then, I have received emails from hundreds of readers who have made a successful transition from eBay to Amazon. This new expanded edition includes some of the more advanced features of Amazon and allows for many of the controversial eBay changes of 2008.

When I registered for eBay in 1999, I couldn't have imagined where it would ultimately lead. Within a year, I was actually employed by eBay. It all happened through a bunch of coincidences and accidental meetings, but it has been a wonderful thing.

In 2002 I left the regular job at eBay and became an eBay University instructor. At the time, there were only six of us, Jim "Griff" Griffith, and Marsha Collier among others. We crisscrossed the country teaching all sorts of people about this phenomenon called eBay. It was an absolute blast.

When I first considered writing this, I felt a little like I was betraying an old friend. It's funny that a lot of long-time eBay sellers feel a lot of emotion about eBay. In fact, I don't think I have ever seen so much emotion between a company, and its customers.

Let me say upfront that this is not a bash-eBay book. I firmly believe sellers need to sell in more than one place. Most sellers agree on that point. It seems to me, offering my stuff to the most people will get me the most sales.

Well, the most people are at eBay and Amazon.

Both sites have pros and cons. I hope you'll figure out what the pros and cons are for both sites – because if you do, you can sell a lot of stuff.

Between the two sites there are over 100 million visitors each month. Figure out the rules, abide by them, and *sell*. Sell smart. Try to avoid negative discussion boards. Concentrate on selling and doing it well.

I'm amazed when I hear people say, "I just can't sell there anymore." I don't buy that. It is possible to sell on eBay, and millions do it every day. It's just not as lucrative or fun as it once was.

Those days are gone. So it's time to get down to business and sell somewhere else.

I am neither an optimist nor pessimist, but a possibilist.
—Max Lerner, *American Journalist*

What to expect from this book

> **"What were the people like where you come from?"**
>
> *Centuries ago a traveler approached a village gate. As he approached, he met an old man sitting in the gate who rose to greet him. The traveler asked, "What kinds of people live in this village? I'm leaving my old village and I'm looking for a new home."*
>
> *The old man asked, "What were the people like where you come from?"*
>
> *The traveler said, "They were awful, rude people. I had no friends; people were trying to cheat me at every turn. I was miserable."*
>
> *The old man said, "I'm sorry my son, the people in this village are exactly the same. You will not be happy here either." The traveler nodded, and then continued on his search.*
>
> *Later the same day, another traveler approached the same gate, with the same old man. The traveler asked, "What kinds of people live in this village? I'm leaving my old village and I'm looking for a new home."*
>
> *The old man asked, "What were the people like where you come from?"*
>
> *The traveler said, "They were wonderful people. I had many good friends, business was strong, and it was a most hospitable village. I wish I didn't have to leave."*
>
> *The old man said, "Welcome, you will be very happy here. The people in this village are just like that. Please come in and stay."*

The moral of that story is: life is what you make of it. If you are moving from eBay because you just can't be happy there, you will likely find the same situation at Amazon.

Amazon is a big corporation, like eBay. They have rules, some grouchy sellers on their discussion boards, and stockholders, like eBay. You are a relatively small seller, dealing with very, very large companies. Keep your perspective, work within the rules, and remember the three P's - professional, polite, and prompt. Applying those principles in all areas of your selling, and you will make money on either site or both.

You may have noticed that the eBay community has a lot of emotion. They get quite upset when eBay makes changes. eBay has allowed business to become very personal with their selling community. Getting caught up in all the emotion clouds judgment and can hurt your business.

Don't let selling on Amazon become emotional. Focus on making money. Follow the rules. Don't try to change them. Look at it as another place to sell your stuff.

Cutting through a jungle of confusion

eBay sellers have a difficult time navigating the Amazon website. Many of us have grown comfortable with eBay's layout and design. Amazon seems like a foreign country. Answers are not always easy to find, terminology is different, and the selling process is different. An Amazon customer service representative even told me "there is no *single* place to go for answers." Let's face it, when you're desperate to make a move, all the research and reading required to navigate a new site is a chore.

By the time you finish this book you should be able to begin listing (and selling) items on Amazon.com. Many people think of Amazon as a bookselling site. It's much, much more than that. Amazon had more shoppers than eBay in the last quarter of 2007. They weren't all buying books.

You're going to learn how to:

- open an account
- list inventory
- price your items
- pack and ship the Amazon way
- make money!

At Amazon I found an entirely different group of buyers. My Amazon buyers are a pleasure to deal with, mostly because I didn't have to deal with them.

Longtime Amazon sellers, have developed sophisticated selling strategies, they know the site backwards and forwards. This book is not written for them. It's written for the small to medium-size eBay seller, who wants to increase their income, by selling to a different market. The average eBay seller doesn't want to run an ever-growing business; they just want to sell some stuff to make extra money.

Chapter 2

Can I Make Money At This?

No doubt you've heard of people selling things on the internet and making money. They may be earning a little "mad money" for a rainy day, or they may make their entire living as an online retailer.

It's all pretty basic Business 101. You offer things people want, at a fair price, and people will buy those things. You deliver the product, and people will come back.

Here are the questions that come up most often:

- **Where will I get things to sell?**

- **How do I know what people want to buy?**

- **How do I set the prices for my items?**

- **How do I ship the things I sell?**

- **Is the Amazon community safe?**

Let's consider these questions right up front, and see how *you* can make money selling online.

Where Will I Get Things to Sell?

As with any business, you'll have to find a source for products to sell online. This could be as "low-tech" as your basement, or garage sales. If you already have established product sources, perhaps from a current or former business, you might be able to use them. Or you may want to explore new avenues to obtain products to sell.

With the increase in small, online businesses over the last few years, there are companies that offer to sell you lists of "wholesalers" that will supposedly help you get products at low cost. Most of these are worthless. Do not send money to them. You will rarely find real wholesalers by doing a search on Google.

Later in this book, I discuss product sourcing a little more. I recommend a company called Worldwide Brands (**http://tinyurl.com/Product-Sourcing**) in large part, because I personally know the founders, and I use them myself.

Rest assured, you will be able to find things to sell. A lot of it depends on what you *want* to sell.

How Do I Know What People Want to Buy?

There are several ways to find this information. Much of it is freely available—you just have to do a little detective work.

On Amazon, you can choose a main category, and on the right side of the page choose *Bestsellers*. Right there you can see what is selling in that category. Watch for trends. Obviously at certain times of the year you will see trends develop. In late summer, you'll see lots of "back to school" items, before holidays, you'll see related trends.

Basically though, people are buying the same things online as they do offline. Be observant of what is being advertised all around you.
As a side note, don't let yourself get caught up in trying to sell the latest "hot" items. There is often little profit in hot, high-ticket items because everyone else is selling them, and the price tends to go down.

Think about what you enjoy, and what you know. If you enjoy cooking, and know a lot about kitchenware, consider that. If you have spent a career as a mechanic, you probably know more about tools than most people. If fly-fishing has been your hobby for the past 30 years, guess what you should sell.

Don't worry as much about what people want to buy, as much as what you can convincingly sell.

How Do I Set Prices For My Items?

This seems harder than it really is. Before you buy any products for resale, you'll need to research similar products and see how much they are selling for. You can look on Amazon.com for hints, but you can also look on other sites such as eBay to get an idea of the market prices.

Obviously you'll need to set your prices so that once the bills are paid, you'll have made a profit for your efforts. It's amazing that many people don't know how much they make on a sale. It's also amazing that many sellers aren't really making money, and they don't even realize it.

You have to calculate the true cost of doing business. The product is not your only cost. There is also your office, supplies, internet service. Don't forget trips to the Post Office, shipping materials, Amazon fees, and on and on. Once you've paid all those things, and you can still see a profit, you're in the ballpark.

One rule to remember is: "Do not compete on price alone." Competing on price will always drive the price down, and you'll ultimately lose to a larger seller every time.

Price your items for what they are worth. Provide outstanding customer service, and quality items, and you will succeed in selling your items.

How Do I Ship the Things I Sell?

When you sell items on Amazon, you'll need to ship them within two business days. The items will need to be properly packed & weighed, postage applied, and shipped.

Where will you do that? You will want to streamline your shipping processes or you'll find yourself running to the office supply store for materials, and back and forth to the Post Office to send the packages.

You'll need a space where you can work. You should have the appropriate, new packaging materials. Depending on what you're shipping, you'll want to have boxes, shipping tubes, or bubble-mailers. You'll probably need a postage scale, which you can find at your local office supply store. You'll also need tape and markers. And you'll want to have it all set up neatly on a nice big work table as a "shipping station."

I'll go into shipping labels and the actual shipping process later on. But you should plan on getting set up to create and print your own shipping labels at home on your existing printer. Then, you can have your postal carrier just pick up your pre-paid packages at your door. No trips to the Post Office!

Is the Amazon community as safe as eBay's community?

The short answer is yes. But you still need to be careful. In any community, there are people that are good and there are scoundrels. It is just as true in the online community.

Common sense is your best defense. Obviously never ship an item until you've been paid. Also, never give anyone access to your accounts. Amazon customer service will never ask you for your password, so if someone does, you know you should not give it out.

There are many sites online where you can sell your things. Amazon is one of the safest. Part of the reason is Amazon collect the payment for you. You won't even know you've sold anything until they have the payment in hand. Then, a couple of times each month, they'll deposit the payments automatically into the checking account that you specify.

Another reason they are safer is you have very little interaction with your buyers. Most Amazon buyers just want to order their product, pay for it, and move on. Since there is less access to you as a seller, the scoundrels tend to move on to easier prey elsewhere.

Just remember, common sense is the key to online safety. A good website for online safety tips from the U.S. Federal Government is: **www.onguardonline.gov**.

Benefits of Multi-channel Selling

Do you have your eggs in one basket?

Multi-channel selling once meant selling some things in "brick and mortar" stores and some things online. Today, online sales have become a multi-channel environment of their own. There are many channels available to the online retailer.

At some time in your life, you have no doubt been warned by some well-meaning person, not to "put your eggs all in one basket." In other words, minimize your risk of loss by separating valuable things. That way it's less likely a single catastrophe will wipe you out.

The principle works for online retailers too. If you sell exclusively on one site, you are at significant risk. Let me ask you: If there was a problem with your eBay or PayPal account – and either one (or both) of those accounts was shut down – would you be out of business?

For many eBay sellers, eBay was their first love. They learned to sell online with eBay. They haven't tried anything else. In fact, many eBay sellers talk about selling on other sites as if it's a dirty little secret. Before writing this book, I asked dozens of sellers if they sell on Amazon.com. They *whispered* their answer to me! *"Yes, but just books."* It was as if they were cheating on their significant other by selling outside eBay!

You can and should limit your risk, but there are other benefits too…

A Larger – and Different Audience

eBay sellers seem to think that the whole world shops on eBay. Sorry, it's not true. When I began selling on Amazon I found something that really surprised me. There are people in the world that just want to buy their item, pay, and get it in the mail. They don't shop on eBay. They don't want to chat on discussion boards, read a cute About Me page, or bid on auctions.

By offering items to eBay buyers *and* Amazon buyers you significantly increase the audience for your products.

Is your goal to expand your sales to Amazon or to leave eBay completely? Let me be clear. Amazon is not a silver bullet for all your selling woes. You will find some Amazon sellers have complaints, just like eBay sellers. Abandoning eBay will simply replace one group of buyers with another. Some things still sell very well on eBay. Other things sell quite well on Amazon. Make both sites work for you.

Selling on only one platform can be stressful. Once I started selling on Amazon, I felt less pressure to "make it work" on eBay. Then I began to view eBay and Amazon simply as tools for selling. It was a relief. I have no doubt you'll feel the same relief.

You are on your way to learning an additional way to sell your stuff, and you can earn very good money.

Why Amazon?

"What about 'eBay alternative' sites?"

You don't have to go far to find many other sites claiming to be the alternative to nasty ol' eBay. I'm going to be blunt here okay? Forget it. There are a few sites like Etsy.com (which specializes in hand-made products) that have a niche and are getting some traction. But eBay and Amazon have the brand and the traffic. Learn to accept that. You need them more than they need you. It hurts to hear the truth. (I'll wait while you grab a tissue...)

<u>Buyers</u> go to eBay. Students in my eBay classes are usually current eBay buyers that want to become sellers. Occasionally I ask them if they've heard about the latest eBay controversy. In return, I usually get blank stares.

Buyers do not care about your problems as a seller. They are not going to band behind you and follow you to the small "alternative" sites. They want selection. If you choose to sell on small sites with little traffic, you will have small sales, if any. Jumping onto a small site to protest eBay policies is like driving exclusively on dirt roads to protest the highway commission's latest policies. Do you really expect to get anywhere doing that?

Another Basket for Your Eggs

Amazon and eBay have grown up together. They both have the high traffic and great brand recognition required to bring buyers to their respective marketplaces. They both have loyal buyers that come back again and again.

Many sellers agree, Amazon buyers are more affluent. As a result, sellers find a higher average selling price for their items on Amazon. I have found this to be true.

There is debate over which site has pickier customers. I have found the Amazon buyers much easier to deal with. I have much less contact with my Amazon customers. They find the item they want, they *pay*, then once payment is confirmed, you receive notice that the item sold and you should ship the item. And...there is no such thing as a non-paying Amazon customer.

The fact is, eBay and Amazon are not the same. eBay has allowed the shopping experience to be a lot about the seller, and then the product. Sellers are encouraged to be creative, stand out from the crowd, and try hard to show up in search results.

The Amazon shopping experience is about the product. Sellers take an almost invisible roll in the process. Amazon is stricter about how sellers present themselves. Shoppers search for a product, and then they get to see which sellers offer that product. In time, you'll see that as a good thing. Once you get the hang of it, selling on Amazon is much easier than selling on eBay.

Look at Amazon as another "basket for your eggs."

Chapter 3

Using What You've Learned on eBay

eBay has worked hard to educate their sellers. Through a variety of methods, both online and offline, they continue to teach average people how to sell merchandise online.

Before eBay, most sellers had little or no understanding about keywords, digital photos, online payments, or packing and shipping. These things are now second nature.

Many of the concepts you learned on eBay, can be used when selling on Amazon. Some of those now-familiar concepts are:

- researching the marketplace
- understanding the importance of keywords
- pricing competitively
- great customer service
- good packaging and shipping practices

Your experience writing eBay descriptions will also pay off on Amazon. Later you will see how optimizing your listings on Amazon will make you stand out, even among seasoned Amazon sellers.

Product Sourcing

If you ask about product sourcing on the Amazon discussion boards, you'll likely get a response suggesting you do that on your own time.

If you have a source for new products for eBay, you should continue to use that source. If you found success on eBay, you probably went in search of more product to sell. One of the best channels for finding distributors that will work with small businesses is Worldwide Brands. The service and advice they give works for eBay, and some sellers have used them to buy merchandise for resale on Amazon too.

Drop shipping may not be an option for you. Amazon orders need to ship within two business days, and drop shipping takes fulfillment out of your hands. However, if you have a little room, you may buy product for resale. If you don't already have a source, I recommend Worldwide Brands. You can visit them at: **http://tinyurl.com/Product-Sourcing**
I use them, and I trust them, what they say works.

Now, let's get started.

Chapter 4

Your Amazon Seller Account

The Amazon Marketplace and Seller Central

When Amazon began, it was primarily a marketplace for books. Eventually other media products were added such as CDs and DVDs. This media area of Amazon is known as the Amazon Marketplace.

There is another area of Amazon known as Seller Central. This area is for sellers who sell primarily *non-media* items. (Non-media items include anything besides Books, CDs, and DVDs.) There are a few differences between the Marketplace and Seller Central. For example, in the Marketplace categories, the amount you can charge for shipping is set by Amazon. When shipping a book for example, you may not charge more than the set rate.

In Seller Central, you cannot list books or other media items. When you do list an item though, you may set the shipping charge for that item. If you're selling a heavy *KitchenAid* Mixer, you can charge accordingly for shipping.

What if you want to sell a book though? In that case, you will need a Marketplace account as well. Two accounts? Yes, even though it's generally a rule that you cannot have two seller accounts, you may have two for a situation like the one described above.

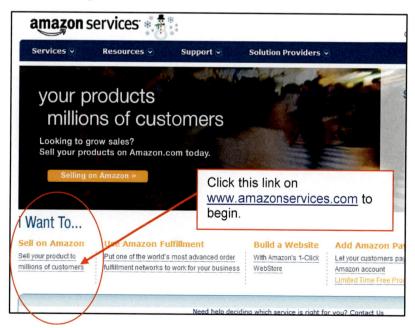

Just make sure you never list anything on Seller Central that you have in the Marketplace account.

So you see the distinction between being a Marketplace seller or a Seller Central seller does not depend on your volume or the *size* of your business, it is determined solely by what you want to sell.

When you are ready to create an Amazon seller account, you'll see a screen with a link that invites you to *"Sell your products to millions of customers."*

Which is best for you?

Before we get too far, let me explain just a little more about Amazon's seller account levels. There are basically two types you can choose from. There are differences that I'll explain more later, but you should know a little more before you sign up.
The most basic account is an individual seller account. Amazon does not charge anything for this type of account. You are allowed to list products that are already listed in Amazon's catalog, at no charge. When your item sells, Amazon charges $.99 per item, plus a commission.
An upgraded account is called a Pro Merchant account. This costs $39.99 per month and Amazon waives the $0.99 fee for each item sold. Besides that, you get some extra tools and permissions.
The bottom line is, if you are planning to sell only a few items or expect to have less than 40 sales a month, you can save money with the individual account. You can always upgrade when you are ready.

Registering as an Amazon Seller

Start by visiting www.amazonservices.com and click the link highlighted on the previous page. You will then see the screen on the next page.

Amazon would like you to set up a Pro Merchant account. They get paid more that way. At this point however, you may want to set up a free individual seller account to get started. To do that, follow the link that says "Click here" in the middle of the first paragraph (as indicated above.)

When you click that link, you'll be asked to list your first item. During the listing process, you'll be prompted to set up the rest of your account. Have an old book, CD, or some other item ready to sell when you begin this process.

As you set up your Seller account, you will need an email address, and a credit (or debit) card ready.

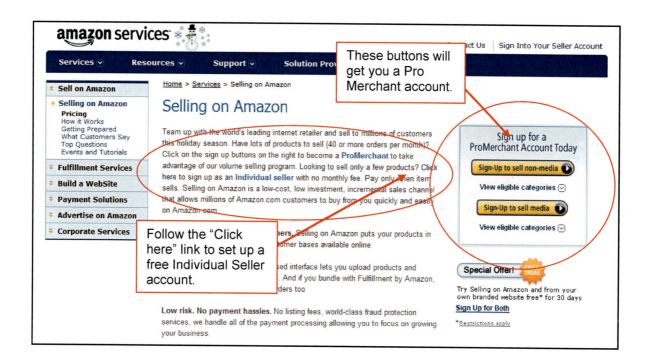

Set up is a quick five-step process. You'll be asked for your email and password first. This will be your login information for Amazon.com. Next you'll get to choose a Display Name. This is basically your seller ID on Amazon.com. It will appear near your items. (It's up to you if you want to try to have your nickname on Amazon match your eBay user ID.)

Next, fill in your address, credit card information, and other personal information. You can always upgrade to a Pro Merchant account later if you'd like. A Pro Merchant account is on a month by month basis, so you can also downgrade if you find you're not selling enough to make it worthwhile.

You will be able to direct people to all of your listings through your *Seller Profile* using a direct URL: http://www.amazon.com/seller/*your-nickname*. (Replace "your-nickname" with your Amazon nickname.) From your *Seller Profile*, users may view your Feedback, and your current listings.

> **FAQ** - *"Why do you need to add a credit card?" When you sell an item on Amazon, they collect the payments from buyers and pay you twice per month. Let's say you sell a book on the 15th, Amazon pays you on the 16th, and for some reason you need to refund the buyer's payment on the 17th. Since Amazon has already passed the payment for that item along to you, your Amazon payment account is empty. In order to refund the buyer, Amazon will deduct the refund from your credit card.*

Seller Fees

Amazon's fee structure is different than eBay's. Many sellers feel that once everything is considered, they are almost equal. You can easily find the Amazon seller fees at: _Help_ > _Selling at Amazon.com_ > _Getting Paid_ > _Fees and Pricing._

Amazon.com collects fees only when your item sells. At that time, Amazon.com collects your sales price and shipping costs from the buyer, deducts a commission of 6 to 15 percent of the sales price, a per-transaction fee of $0.99, and a variable closing fee. The commission varies based on the category in which your item sells.

The fees may <u>seem</u> higher than eBay at first, but consider some differences:

- there are no listing fees – if your item doesn't sell, you don't pay
- you spend less time listing and relisting items that didn't sell
- Amazon collects the payment for you – no chasing non-paying buyers
- Amazon deposits your payments directly into your checking account – no PayPal fees
- average selling prices tend to be higher on Amazon – you make more money

The Product Detail Page – a Fundamental Difference

Each product for sale on Amazon has a *product detail page*. This is the page that shows all the details about the product for sale. Everyone who sells this *exact* product uses the same page. A seller locates the page for their product, and adds their name to the list of sellers offering that item. They can add unique comments to their listing called "Condition notes." Adding an item to an existing product page is called by some a "Me too" listing.

Amazon is quite different from eBay in this area. Think of adding a page to Amazon as adding a product to a catalog. There should be only one unique page for each product. Amazon wants the product detail page to be a neutral page for the product, you can add other details later when you sell an item, but the actual product page is not a place to get cute and creative. When other sellers sell an identical product, they will use the product detail page you create. This is a new concept for eBay sellers. Just remember, the *product detail page* is not "your" page. It is *not* the equivalent of a listing page on eBay.

Imagine if you had red hats to sell. No one has ever sold them on Amazon before. To sell your red hats you will have to add them to Amazon's catalog. So you create a *product detail page* that basically tells Amazon, "This product exists, it's *this* big, made of *this* material, and it's made by *X-Y-Z company*." That's it. Now the Red Hat is in the Amazon catalog. But no one is selling it yet.

To sell your red hats, you find the *product detail page* and basically tell Amazon, "I have one of those hats to sell." You can then add yourself as a seller of Red Hats and set your price, and list your items. (I'll cover this in much more detail a little later.) When you actually add your Red Hat to be sold, you'll have an opportunity to describe it in detail in the "condition notes."

Once you get used to Amazon's process, it's much easier than eBay. It seems *too* easy.

"So?" you ask, "Can just anyone create a *product detail page*?" No, they must pay for the privilege. There are various levels of seller accounts. Let's look at the most common types.

Amazon Seller Account Levels

Individual Seller

Whether you sell in the Marketplace, or Seller Central, this is the most basic seller account at Amazon. An Amazon Individual Seller can list items for sale using an <u>existing</u> Amazon *product detail page*. For example, if you find a used book you'd like to sell, and it is currently being sold, or has been sold on Amazon, you simply find the book, and click the *Sell yours here* button in the upper right-hand column, and list your item using the existing *product detail page*. Listings automatically expire after 60 days and can be relisted through your Seller Account.

What if you have merchandise that is *not* already in the Amazon marketplace? In that case you'll need to upgrade.

Amazon Pro Merchant Subscription

If the item you'd like to sell is not included in Amazon's vast array of existing products, do not despair. You can upgrade your seller account to what is known as a Pro Merchant subscription for a monthly fee (currently $39.99).

With your Pro Merchant subscription, you will be able to create your own *product detail pages*. As we've learned, this allows you to sell items not currently found in the Amazon catalog.

Amazon waives the $0.99 transaction fee per sold item for Pro Merchant sellers. Also, your item listings won't expire after 60 days, but will stay active indefinitely!

How will you know whether to spring for a Pro Merchant subscription? If you're selling enough to justify $39.99 per month, it opens up opportunities for you to sell your own unique items. If you're selling 40 items per month, and paying the $0.99 fee for each item, you can break even as a Pro Merchant. There are more benefits than just cost. Pro Merchant benefits include:

- **Save $0.99 per sale**

- **List and update inventory using volume listing tools**

- **Create your own personalized storefront featuring only your items**

- **Create your own product pages in the Amazon.com catalog**

- **Listings that don't expire**

Amazon Merchants

Yet another account type is the Amazon Merchant. These large merchants have a special relationship with Amazon. They are generally larger retailers such as Eddie Bauer, Office Depot, or Macy's. They have more control over their presence on Amazon (and probably will not be reading this book). These are the big boys.

Category Restrictions

You should know that Amazon controls access to certain categories. Sellers of collectibles understand that their buyers find items primarily by searching, not by browsing. Find the most appropriate Everything Else sub-category. Then, list your item. You can find plenty of sellers offering *vintage* and *collectible* items. Just do a search on Amazon and see what other sellers are doing.

Sellers in the restricted (or *gated*) categories must be approved by Amazon to create product pages. Only the most qualified merchants are allowed to sell in these categories. Retailers most likely to be approved are sellers that bring additional value to the category by means of their product selection, brand, and pricing. Occasionally, Amazon will base restrictions on the current amount of a particular product within a category. This helps approved sellers avoid too much supply within their category which tends to drive prices into the ground.

Before you lay out money for a Pro Merchant upgrade, see if you can sell your merchandise on Amazon. Here is a list of open and restricted categories:

Open Categories

- Automotive
- Baby Products
- Books / Video / Music
- Computer and Video Games
- Electronics
- Home Kitchen and Garden
- Everything Else
- Musical Instruments
- Office Products
- Pet Supplies
- Software
- Sporting Goods
- Tools and Hardware
- Toys and Games

Restricted or "Gated" Categories

- Apparel and Accessories
- Beauty
- Cell phones and Plans
- Gourmet Food
- Jewelry and Watches
- Magazines
- Health and Professional Care

You'll notice that *Toys and Games* is in both boxes. This is because around the winter holiday season, this category may become temporarily restricted. For example, this year Amazon prevented new sellers from selling in the *Toys and Games* category from September 12th through January 5th. Existing *Toys and Games* sellers who did not meet certain performance requirements were unable to list in this category from November 17th through January 5th.

"How Do I Get Approved to Sell in a Restricted Category?"

There is no published "process" to get onto the list of approved sellers. The restrictions are category-specific.

Amazon handles this on a case by case basis based on contracts they have with other sellers or the risk involved with certain merchandise. One good thing is, in most cases, real humans determine permissions.

To ask permission to sell in a gated category, you can use the contact form found at: www.amazonservices.com/semland/contact.

What are they looking for when considering giving permission? They may want to see that you're a legitimate business; they may want to see your listings on other sites such as eBay, or other parts of Amazon. They may also look for a track record of adherence to Amazon's policies, honesty, and good customer service.

If you are just starting out, get established with non-gated categories before asking for permission to sell in the restricted categories.

The fact that Amazon controls access to some categories is really of benefit to you as a seller. It helps buyers develop trust and draws them back. Once you are granted permission, you can sell to those buyers.

The Pre-order Report

As a general rule, Amazon does not provide lists of completed sales. There is another great resource available to sellers who have a Pro Merchant account. It's called the Buyer's Waiting List.

If a product is not available on Amazon, buyers may pre-order it from the product detail page, and indicate how much they're willing to pay once it's available. Once it becomes available they are notified and can purchase the item.

A caution: just because someone says they're waiting doesn't mean they have to buy an item when it becomes available. In fact, you cannot see who put the item on the Buyer's Waiting List.

That being said, the list does show products that are scarce, for which people will sometimes pay big bucks. I use the list to do a little shopping on those smaller sites. Many people on other sites underprice their items. You can pick them up for a steal and list them on Amazon where the supply is lower.

If you have an Amazon Pro Merchant subscription, you can logon and download the Pre-order Report. It may be opened using MS Excel or another spreadsheet program.

To get the most recent Pre-order Report go to: *Help > Ordering > Amazon Marketplace > Pre-Orders.*

Chapter 5

Classifying Your Product

The folks at Amazon have millions of products to keep organized. As sellers add products to the Amazon catalog, they are asked to categorize or "classify" them.

If your item already exists in the Amazon catalog, you are supposed to use the existing *Product Detail Page* to list your product. Over time, some sellers have ignored this rule, and the result is multiple Product Detail Pages for the same exact item. This is known as "catalog pollution."

The result of catalog pollution is the shopper gets mixed results. For example, as of this writing, if you search specifically for *KitchenAid Mixers & Attachments Recipes & Instructions* you'll get five results, all for the same spiral-bound book. Which is best? They should all be selling on one Product Detail Page.

The Universal Product Code (UPC)

Back in 1974 grocery stores started using a funny looking bar code called a UPC or Universal Product Code. It was developed for grocery stores, but has become—as the name implies—universal.

Products from mixers to radiator hoses are classified and identified by a UPC. It's not perfect, but it is the best solution for now.

In order to offer a more organized marketplace to their shoppers, Amazon has begun requiring a UPC when creating a new Product Detail Page. This requirement is rolling out gradually but expect it to be, well, *universal* in the near future.

The good news is just about anything you can imagine is already in the Amazon catalog. If a *Product Detail Page* has already been created by another seller, you can piggy-back on that page with your product For example, if you have acquired a *Black & Decker F930 Light 'N Easy Smart-Steam Nonstick Iron* and you'd like to sell it on Amazon, you can simply type in the UPC and click *Sell yours here*.

"I Create One-of-a-Kind Items, with No UPC, Can I Sell on Amazon?"

Amazon realizes that some things will not have a UPC, and it can be too expensive for small sellers to get one for each individual product. For those cases, you can request an exemption for your product.

Recently, I heard from a lady who makes baby quilts. Each one is unique, so she would have to have a UPC for every single product. A UPC can cost anywhere from $6 to around $50. This was obviously not something she could recover in her retail price. So she was in dire need of an exemption. Since there is little chance anyone else would ever create the exact items she was making, she should be able to get exempted from this rule.

Exemptions are category dependent. The Amazon staff dealing with each category is aware of which products will, or will not, have UPCs. They also know when a seller should be able to get UPCs.

They only allow exemptions for specific reasons. So make sure you qualify before making your request. Here are the basic reasons they consider valid:

- **Private label**: Non-nationally branded product on your own company's label

- **Specialized**: Low-volume accessory part/item with a specialized function

- **Non-consumer**: A business-to-business product not sold in a retail store

- **Pre-configured**: Made-to-order or custom products

For more information go to: https://sellercentral.amazon.com/gp/help/48551.

How to Get a UPC Code for Your Products

Items such as antiques, handmade items, or other items without a UPC can still be sold on Amazon.com. If you have such an item, and you have a Pro-Merchant subscription, you can still create a Product Details Page using the *Everything Else* category. A word of caution though: If your item SHOULD have a UPC and there is a category specifically for it on Amazon, you may not use the *Everything Else* category as a work-around. In other words, don't try to cheat.

Everything Else means *everything other than categorized items*. Amazon is pretty strict about keeping the site well organized.

There are two things you can do to try to get around the UPC requirement. First, you can talk with a rep on the phone. If you've been frustrated with eBay phone support, you'll be happy with Amazon. From your Manage Your Inventory Page, in the upper right click *Seller Help* and have Amazon call you. Then ask them what you should do to be able to list your item.

Second, if you hit the UPC wall, you can email Amazon and ask for an exception to the rule for your product. There is a good chance you can get one if you make your case well. Be polite, and don't get nasty if you can't get an exception right now. They assure me they are working on a number of things to accommodate the large number of eBay sellers beginning to sell there. (I predict a *Collectibles* category in the future—you heard it here first.)

Here is some information directly from Amazon that you should find helpful:

Currently, we require a Universal Product Code (UPC) or a European Article Numbers (EAN) for many products submitted through our Create a Product Detail Page feature. We require this identifying data for the following products:

- *Baby Products (UPC or EAN)*
- *Camera & Photo (UPC or EAN)*
- *Computer & Video Games (UPC or EAN)*
- *Electronics (UPC or EAN)*
- *Home, Kitchen & Garden (UPC or EAN)*
- *Music CD or Cassette (UPC or EAN)*
- *Musical Instruments (UPC or EAN)*
- *Software (UPC or EAN)*
- *Tools & Hardware (UPC or EAN)*
- *Toys & Games (UPC or EAN)*
- *Video & DVD (UPC)*

If the item you would like to sell falls under one of the categories listed above and does not have the required product identifier, it cannot be listed using the Create a Product Detail Page feature. However, if the item being sold was manufactured or printed prior to the establishment of UPC codes, you can write to our Seller Performance group to request permission to create the catalog page without the UPC. You can contact this department via email using the following address:
seller-performance@amazon.com

For more information on obtaining a UPC or EAN, please contact:

Uniform Code Council Inc.
8163 Old Yankee Road, Suite J
Dayton, OH 45458 USA
Telephone: (937) 435-3870
www.gs1us.org

(Help > Selling at Amazon.com > Experienced and Volume Selling > Create a Product Page > Requirements & Restrictions)

How Do I Request an UPC Exemption?

The request must be made through Seller Central (not Marketplace). The steps are fairly straightforward:

- Click the link at the bottom of any page that says *Get technical support.*

- In the contact form, for the topic, choose *Other question or request.*

- In the Short Description field, type: UPC EXEMPTION REQUEST—*Your merchant name.*

- In the body, list your products, or if you have a large number of products, list some products that represent your catalog. This list should include brands, any relevant descriptions, and the total number of items for which you need exemptions.

- For each item, you'll need to explain why there won't be a UPC.

Chapter 6

Creating a Product Detail Page

Four Steps to Creating a *New* Product Detail Page

If you're an Amazon Pro Merchant, you can create a brand new product detail page. If the item you sell isn't in Amazon's catalog, you can add it.

There are four main steps to create a product page for the item you want to sell.

1. Classify the product
2. Identify the product
3. Add details
4. Sell your product

I recommend you read through steps 1 – 4 below, and then watch the video tutorial at the end.

To begin creating your product detail page, start at Amazon.com, click the *"Your Account"* **link in the upper right corner of the page. Then click the** *"Your Seller Account"* **link on the right side of the page under "Marketplace."**

Under the "Manage Your Inventory" heading, click the link that says *"Create a product detail page."*

STEP 1: Classify Your Product

Type a few simple keywords into the search box to determine the proper category for your product. For best results, use basic words about the product. This page will seem familiar to eBay sellers, since it's similar to eBay's category finder. Use the *"Search for your product's category"* box to locate the category classification for the product you want to add to Amazon. Or just as with eBay, you can browse the categories and subcategories to choose the best one on your own.

> *TIP: Choosing the best category ensures you'll see the most appropriate data fields for your product in the next steps. It will also place your product where buyers find similar items in the Amazon catalog. Don't try to be clever here, put your item in the proper category.*

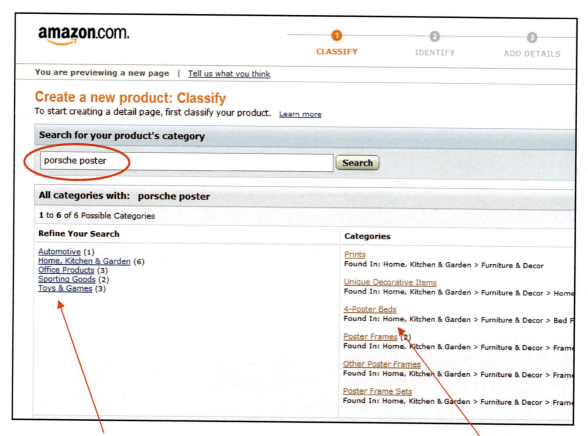

The list on the left gives a list of high-level subcategories with similar products. The results page suggests a list of product categories on the right. You can drill down in these categories to find just the right one for your product.

STEP 2: Identify Your Product

Now that you've classified your product with a category, you need to identify it for Amazon. The more information you supply in this step, the easier it will be for shoppers to find your product.

In other words, you've told Amazon, "I have <u>something</u> to sell in the Home, Kitchen & Garden category. Now you're going to tell them what it is.

"We Found a Match…"

If you try to create a product page for a product that is already in Amazon's catalog, you'll get this screen:

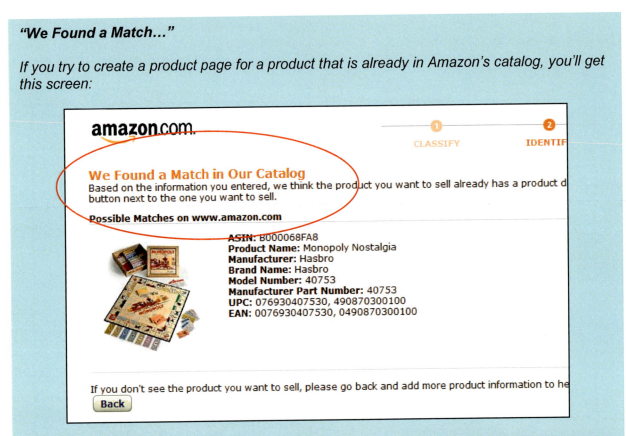

In that case, don't try to work around the existing page and create a duplicate. That's a good way to get punished by Amazon. Use the existing page if you are selling an identical product.

Writing a Great Title

Amazon has a formula they want you to use when writing a title for a new product detail page. They prefer you start with the brand and list the product name. Other things that may be mentioned in the title are quantity (if more than one), color, pattern, model number, power output, and size.

Amazon suggests this **default title style** as a start, then work to make it specific to your product category: *Brand + Model + Product Type*

In addition to the formulas for individual categories, there are several style guidelines that apply to all product categories:

- Capitalize the first letter of each word
- Spell out measure words such as Ounce, Inch, and Pound
- All numbers should be numerals
- Ampersands should not be used in titles unless part of a brand name; spell out and lowercase "and"
- If the size is not a relevant detail, do not list it in the title
- If the product does not come in multiple colors, the color should not be noted in the title

Each category has a slightly different format for titles. Visit Amazon Seller Help for more details on title formats.

You must supply a Product Name, and a Brand Name. In my case, I have a product which is easy to name, but I have no brand name for it. If you have no brand name you'll still need to enter something. I entered my business name, since I'm the first retailer of this product.*

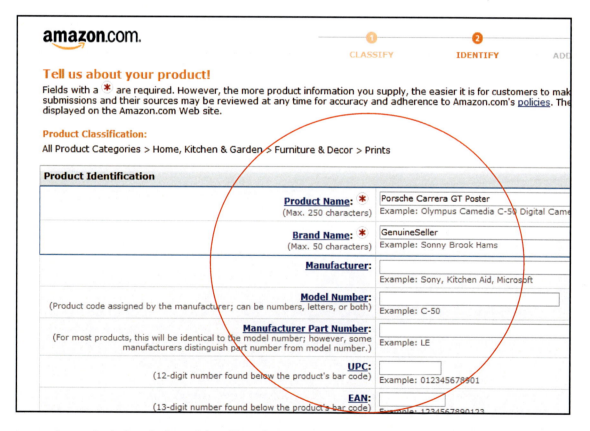

*Amazon reviews submissions to the catalog. There is no guarantee your product will show up after you've submitted it.

STEP 3: Add the Details

Since your product is new to Amazon.com, you are asked to provide identifying information for the catalog before adding descriptive details. This is a little different than an eBay listing. The information should be about the product in general, not your particular item. (Details specific to your particular item will be added later.)

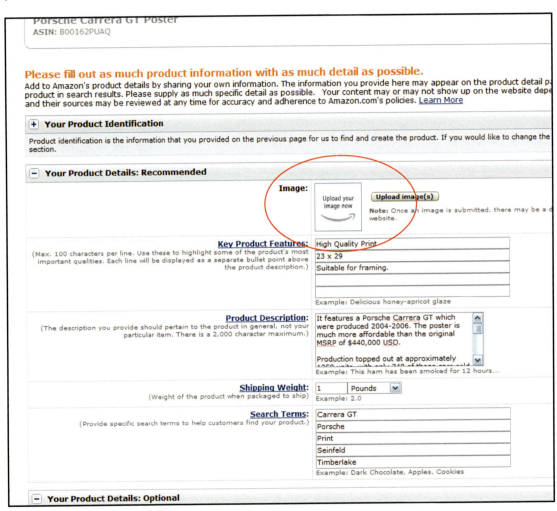

First, you can add an image for your item. Amazon has strict rules about your images. Your image will represent everyone else that has this identical product for sale.

> *FYI:* You cannot have watermark or copyright in your image. Amazon has strict standards for what is contained in images. Since this image will be used to represent this product for all sellers, not just you – you may not put identifying elements within your images. Don't break the rules or you run the risk of having your item removed.

Uploading images is easy. Click the *"Upload image(s)"* button and you'll see a place where you can browse and upload an image from your computer. The page looks like this:

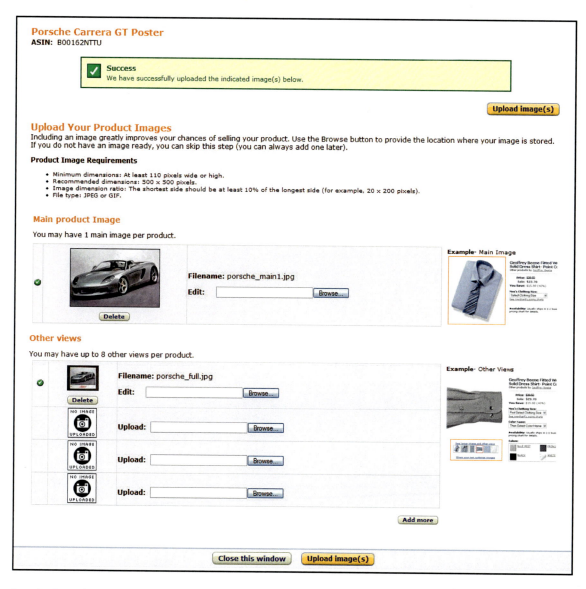

I uploaded a nice cropped image of my poster, and also one showing the full sheet which will need to be trimmed.

Amazon's basic image requirements are:

- The image must be the cover art or a professional photograph of the product being sold. Drawings or illustrations of the product are not allowed.
- The image must not contain gratuitous or confusing additional objects.
- The image must be in focus, professionally lit and photographed or scanned, with realistic color, and smooth edges.
- Books, Music, and Video/DVD images should be the front cover art, and fill 100% of the image frame. Jewel cases, promotional stickers, and cellophane are not allowed.
- All other products should fill 85% or more of the image frame.

- The full product must be in frame.
- Backgrounds must be pure white.
- The image must not contain additional text, graphics, or inset images.
- Pornographic and offensive materials are not allowed.

They're not fooling around. Follow the rules and you'll be fine.

Now back to the details...

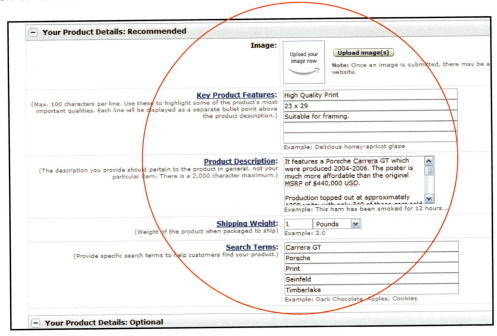

A good detail page will contain all the information a buyer wants to know. Some products need more details than others. You should try to add as much as you can.

Amazon actually has it written in their guidelines that a Product Detail Page must have proper punctuation, capitalized words, and sentence structure. Some eBay sellers have *very* sloppy writing habits. All caps is a no-no, <u>no</u> caps is a no-no, and misspellings are not permitted. Use what you learned in school, write well. Your *product detail page* could be rejected if you fail to follow these guidelines.

Key Product Features: These should be major features of your product. When a shopper looks at your finished product page, they will see these as bullet points. Some shoppers won't scroll very far, so the bullets are an important way to catch their eye.

Features that make good bullet points are:

- Full contents of what's in the box
- Materials and construction
- Major features and benefits
- Details on pattern or design
- Power output
- Dimensions
- Warranty information

These are not the only things, but a good guide when adding Key Product Features. NOTE: This is *not* the place to add remarks about celebrity signatures, additional accessories, extended warranties, where you will or will not ship or condition.

Product Description: In this area you'll discuss the major features of the product in more detail, but without expressing an opinion. Do *not* add things like, "I love this product! It works great!" There is a separate place on the product page for reviews, so keep your opinions to yourself for now.

As an example of what should appear in the product description, you may look at the manufacturer's website. Just don't copy what you see there word for word. You can expand on the bullet points listed above.

Amazon says if in doubt about how much information to include in the product description, err on the side of too much. Many new products don't have reviews to help shoppers make a decision, so your description may be all the help they will get.

This is all you need for an average product, but as you'll see on the page, there is room for much more optional information. This can be filled out at your discretion, but in most cases, you won't need it.

Now, submit the details and move to the actual selling process. It came as a surprise to me that my new page was not searchable right away. It may take up to four days for your newly created page to show up when a shopper performs a search on Amazon.

This new *product detail page* has added a generic "slot" to the catalog. But no items are available for purchase yet. At this point, if a person could see the page we've created they would see the product as "Currently unavailable." Amazon knows the product exists, but no one has said "Hey I want to sell one of those." That's your next step.

STEP 4: Sell

Listing an Item for Sale Using Your Shiny New Product Page

Once you've created your product detail page, you will see the finished page and be offered a chance to sell that item. You can do this by clicking the "Sell yours here" button which begins the listing process.

This is the place where you can get a little more personal about your item. It's also the place where you can differentiate yourself from the crowd of other sellers.

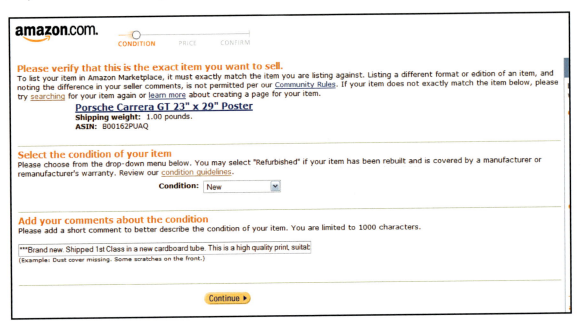

First, there is the *Condition*, choose the appropriate condition of your item from the drop-down box provided. You will have a choice of *New*, and several grades of *Used*. In each category, Amazon provides *condition guidelines* to help you decide which condition to choose. Be honest with your buyers, and with yourself. Do not overestimate the condition of your item. For example, you may have a 100 year old book, and the cover is loose. In your opinion, it's in very good condition for a 100 year old book. Your opinion doesn't matter. Rate the book strictly according to Amazon's condition guidelines. Use them very literally in all categories, or you may be seeing returns on your items.

Now that you've chosen the condition, you finally get to tell people about your particular item.

The Condition Note Attribute – Learn it, love it.

If you are an eBay seller, or an ex-eBay seller, you're probably wondering, "Hey, when can I cut loose with my own words about my fabulous item? I want to *stand out* from all the other sellers."

In the Condition Note attribute you're invited to add your comments about the condition of your item using up to 1,000 characters. This is where you can set your buyer's expectations about your item's condition and detail what is and is not included.

On the next page you'll see a screenshot of an Amazon page with results for a **"Black & Decker Brew 'n' Go Personal Coffee Maker with Travel Mug"**.

At the top are "Featured Merchants" – high level sellers that have an arrangement with Amazon for those spots. Below them are the "New" items, and farther below is the sole "Used" item for this product.

Take note of the "Seller Information" column. You'll see that the Featured Merchants have their logo, rating, and shipping information, but no comments on the product. These big sellers are missing an opportunity to stand out from the competition.

Moving down the page we see items listed by a variety of sellers. Notice their comments in the Condition Attribute box.

Which one is most persuasive to you? The first one circled has comments that apply to that specific product and draws attention to the seller's positive feedback. They also say they ship the same day. (Amazon requires items be shipped within two business days of the sale.)

Other sellers cut corners by having a boring comment that just kind of lays there. This is a missed opportunity for the seller to stand out from the crowd.

The seller of the used item calls out, "NO MUG, NO MUG" to set expectations for the buyer.

The bottom line is: if you are an online retailer selling new products on Amazon, the Condition Attribute is a tremendous opportunity at the *ad level* to differentiate yourself from the other sellers.

> ***TIP***: Once a shopper has gotten to this page, they've probably already decided to make a purchase. You need to be the most persuasive and you will get the sale. Remember: buyers appreciate an honest, literate, informative, and crisp description of the item.

(I know the screenshot on the next page is a little hard to read. You can zoom in on it with the small "+" sign in your Adobe toolbar. Or you can click on the image and see it in your browser.)

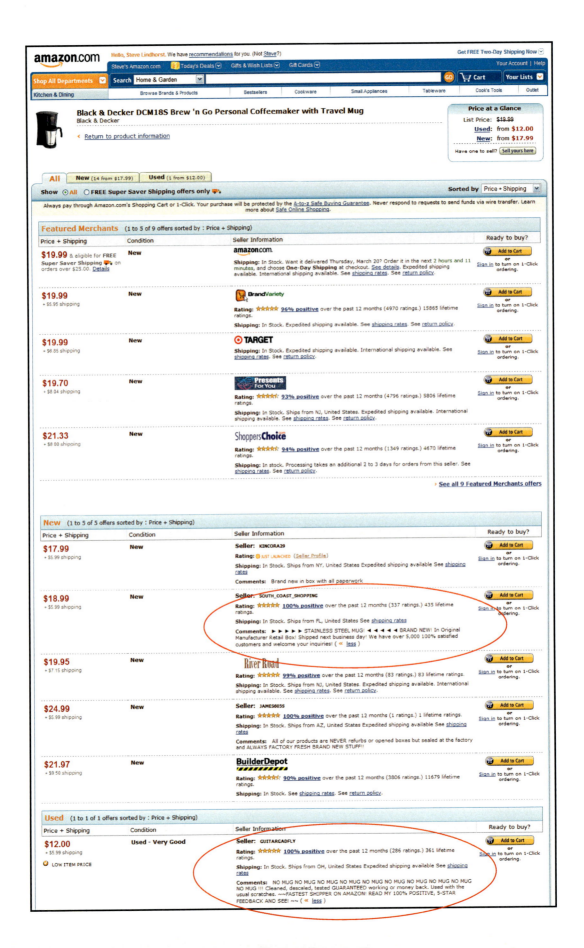

Condition Notes Best Practices

1. Differentiate your message.

   - Look at your competition, and then do something different. If they all mention their warranty, point out your speedy shipping time or 100% feedback.

   - One seller included "Se habla Espanol" to show that they provide multi-language customer support. Another mentioned the fact that their products are not "refurbished."

2. Highlight your business credentials.

   - Indicate that you are a real business. Amazon buyers are not charmed by people shipping from their garage. "Ships direct from our warehouse" has a professional ring to it.

   - Have you received recognition in your field? An award or certificate of achievement? Make sure to use that in your notes.

3. Mention your shipping service.

   - Do you provide a tracking number with your sales? Which shipper will you use? Let shoppers know upfront. You should over-communicate to instill confidence in them as they browse.

4. Combine product and company messaging.

   - Mention accessories that may be overlooked in the Product Detail Page information.

   - Say how long you've been selling these particular products.

   - A few listings included "Authorized resellers" which indicates trust from the big manufacturer. Buyers love that.

Things to Avoid in Your Condition Notes

1. This is *not* eBay

    o Don't waste time saying things like "Powerseller!," "L@@K!," or "ships from a smoke-free home," or "A++++ SELLER!!" here – it sounds unprofessional. It is assumed (especially if the item is rated as "new") that it will not smell like…well, *anything.*

2. Don't use the Condition Notes to repeat the title

    o By the time a shopper finds your item, they know what they're looking at. Also, this is absolutely not the place to let shoppers know that you have something *close* to what's on the product detail page.

3. Do not try to change Amazon's policies

    o One example I saw said "No returns accepted" – sorry, but Amazon offers an A-z guarantee, like it or not you will accept returns if Amazon says you will, or you can go back to eBay. (I'll cover the A-z guarantee a little later.)

    o All third-party sellers on Amazon are bound by the same regulations.

I'd like to give credit to Amazon Strategies for teaching me to look at the condition notes as a way to differentiate yourself on Amazon. It is a great site and you should visit there often for up to date information on Amazon Selling.

Now that we have discussed the Condition and the Condition Notes attribute, we can move to pricing and shipping options.

Chapter 7

Pricing Strategies & Shipping Options

Pricing items on Amazon can be challenging for a seller coming from eBay. The familiar "completed items search" from eBay does not exist on Amazon. Prices are fixed, but where do you set your prices? If you compete on price alone, you may as well just pack up and head back to eBay. It won't work here. I've found two things to be true: you have to be realistic, and patient.

First, Amazon shoppers must consider whether they will buy new, or used. Then, if they will purchase used, they must choose which condition sub-level is acceptable.

Set a price appropriate to the condition of your item. You can see how other sellers have priced the item and use that as a guide. Make sure you "compare apples and apples" though.

If you set your condition as *Used-Very Good* and set your price the same as a *New* book, you probably won't sell your product. Why would a person pay the new price for a used item? On the other hand, don't drag the market down by selling a *Used-Very Good* item at the price of a *Used-Acceptable item*. Get it?

Look at the *Price at a Glance* box on the right side of the Merchant Sellers Page. If I'm selling a used item, I'll click the *"## Used"* link to see prices for other used items. Sometimes I find that the lowest price item is nowhere near as good as mine. I look for similar condition, and a seller with decent feedback. That's my guide for a starting price. But it's only a guide.

Price at a Glance
List Price: $19.99
New: from **$15.99**
Used: from **$20.00**
Have one to sell? [Sell yours here]

It's common for new sellers – especially those who come from eBay – to try to have the lowest price all the time. They have the idea that this will guarantee a sale. Nothing could be further from the truth. Do not compete solely on price. Many other factors help shoppers make a choice. I sell items quite regularly even though I don't have the lowest price. You want to appear confident and be taken seriously. Undercutting a price isn't the way to achieve that. Most of all, by pricing too low, you are shortchanging yourself. Remember, this is about making money.

Below is an example of a pricing page:

![Amazon pricing page screenshot]

Amazon Sales Rank

Amazon provides Sales Rank for products to show how items in their catalog are selling. One place it can be found is at the bottom of the Pricing Details box. The lower the number, the higher the sales for that particular item. The calculation is based on Amazon.com sales and is updated each hour to reflect recent and historical sales of every item sold on Amazon.com.

I know some sellers try to use this to figure out an item's actual sales. But many factors help determine this number. It's not a practical way to determine market demand.

You can use Sales Rank to determine how aggressive you will be with your prices. If the sales rank is a low number (high demand) you can get a little better price. If the sales rank is a high number (low demand) you may want to lower your expectations accordingly if you want to sell your item quickly.

Sales Rank is interesting, but I don't pay much attention to it when choosing *what* to sell. (Some big sellers may argue that point, but I just made $75 on two books ranked over 100,000 while I wrote the last paragraph. If I'd have seen they were ranked that poorly, I may have passed them up.)

> *FYI: Penny Books*
>
> *While it may not affect you if you're not a bookseller, the practice of marking common books (and other media products) at $.01 is very annoying to many sellers on Amazon. It is generally believed that sellers who do this are trying to make a buck on shipping and do so in high volume.*
>
> *A word to the wise: not only do other sellers not like this practice, buyers don't like it either. They know what these sellers are doing and they don't appreciate it. In my research I have run across dozens of messages where buyers say they won't buy from penny booksellers because they don't trust them.*
>
> *Set the price for your product at what it's worth, and be patient*

Autopricers / Undercutting / Price Cutters

Many of the larger sellers on Amazon use software programs to automatically adjust their prices. This is referred to as "autopricing." Autopricing programs constantly scan to ensure the seller has the lowest price on a given product. The program automatically re-prices his item so he has the lowest price. Sometimes this means having the lowest price by one cent.

If your goal is to always maintain the lowest price, you're fighting a losing battle. Trying to keep up with autopricers will quickly result in a dramatic drop in your item's list price.

The best advice I've heard is to stop worrying about being listed first (lowest price). When a buyer clicks on the 'Buy it Used' page, she has most likely already determined to purchase the item. You don't need to worry about *drawing* the customer in with a low price, as you would have on eBay. Convince the shopper that you are the seller they should choose, they will happily pay your asking price.

Some sellers purposely set their prices one cent *above* their competitors. This serves two purposes. First, it doesn't set off the autopricing programs; second, it gives the impression their competition is an undercutter. Since some buyers have stated they dislike undercutting, they will pass up anyone who appears to be doing it. It's an interesting strategy for sure.

Setting Your Price

You should now have enough info to set your price. You'll get a better feel for pricing in time, so don't get too wrapped up in the perfect price. If you have experience with eBay's "Buy It Now" pricing, this should be pretty easy for you. Determine the value of your item, set your price and let it go. In time you can make adjustments if sales are low.

Shipping on Amazon

Shipping is another area of difference between Amazon and eBay. On eBay, you choose when you'll ship your sold items. On Amazon you are expected to ship that item within two business days (weekends and holidays excepted). Period.

You may be used to using shipping as a selling tool, or as a way to make a little extra on each sale. In case you haven't heard, that's next to impossible on Amazon.

Amazon sets the rate for Standard Shipping of your item. They charge the buyer, and pay you a shipping credit to help cover your shipping cost. The rates usually cover the least expensive way to send the package.

Sometimes the shipping credit doesn't cover your entire shipping cost. *You are still required to ship the item to your buyer even if the shipping credit does not fully cover your shipping cost.* You cannot ask the buyer for more money. It's one of those non-negotiable points that Amazon sellers deal with. If you absolutely can't deal with this, you should not sell on Amazon. Remember; don't try to change Amazon, no whining. Work with the system. If you are making a profit when you sell your item, don't worry about losing a little on the shipping. Look at your overall profit and decide if you can make money with the product.

You will be allowed to offer "Expedited Shipping" and "International Shipping." You will receive additional credit for this, but the same holds true – it may not completely cover all of your costs. You are expected to account for any differences in your sale price.

The shipping credit varies by category. Use the table below to determine the amount of your shipping credit if your item sells:

Category	Domestic Standard	Domestic Expedited	International Standard
Books	$3.99	$6.99	$12.49
Music	$2.98	$5.19	$6.89
Videos	$2.98	$5.19	$12.29
DVDs	$2.98	$5.19	$12.29
Video Games	$3.99	$6.99	Not available
Software & Computer Games	$3.99	$6.99	Not available
Electronics	$4.49 + $0.50/lb.*	$6.49 + $0.99/lb.*	Not available
Camera & Photo	$4.49 + $0.50/lb.*	$6.49 + $0.99/lb.*	Not available
Tools & Hardware	$4.49 + $0.50/lb.*	$6.49 + $0.99/lb.*	Not available

Kitchen & Housewares	$4.49 + $0.50/lb.*	$6.49 + $0.99/lb.*	Not available
Outdoor Living	$4.49 + $0.50/lb.*	$6.49 + $0.99/lb.*	Not available
Computer	$4.49 + $0.50/lb.*	$6.49 + $0.99/lb.*	Not available
Sports & Outdoors	$4.49 + $0.50/lb.*	$6.49 + $0.99/lb.*	Not available
Cell Phones & Service	$4.49 + $0.50/lb.*	$6.49 + $0.99/lb.*	Not available
Musical Instruments	$4.49 + $0.50/lb.*	$6.49 + $0.99/lb.*	Not available
Office Products	$4.49 + $0.50/lb.*	$6.49 + $0.99/lb.*	Not available
Toy & Baby	$4.49 + $0.50/lb.*	$6.49 + $0.99/lb.*	Not available
Everything Else	$4.49 + $0.50/lb.*	$6.49 + $0.99/lb.*	Not available

*Refers to the weight of the item, excluding the seller's packaging.

(Table and shipping info source: Amazon.com)

"Standard Shipping" (at least for media products) generally means USPS Media Mail. If you offer Expedited Shipping, and your buyer chooses it, you are expected to ship using a faster service. Many sellers specify they will ship using USPS Priority Mail for Expedited Shipping, but you may use another fast service if you wish.

Note: If you take an Expedited Shipping credit, do not ship via Media Mail and pocket the difference. You are risking suspension from Amazon, and the buyer has every right to report you.

Let's continue to the *Confirm* page...

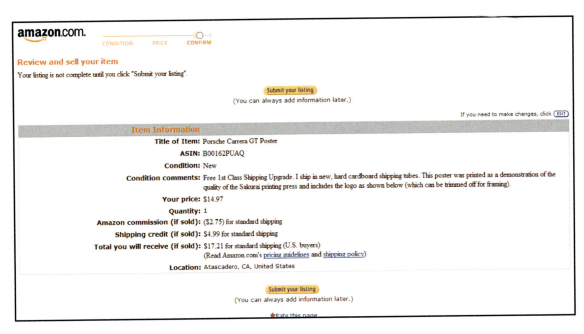

Pretty basic stuff here. Just review what you've done, and submit your listing. It will appear in your inventory and you can edit it more there if necessary.

Video: Creating a Product Detail Page

I have created a video of the entire process you've just read. It's about 15 minutes or so, and you can watch it by typing the following the link into your web browser:

http://www.sellingontheriver.com/vids/amazon_listing/amazon_listing.html

Video: Creating a "Me Too" Listing

I have created a video of the process of adding your item to an existing product detail page. It's about 10 minutes, and you can watch it by typing the following the link into your web browser:

http://www.sellingontheriver.com/vids/amazon_metoo/amazon_metoo.html

"Me too" listings

Anyone with a basic Amazon Seller account can create a listing from an existing product detail page.

Search for your product and find an *exact match* for your item. Then click the "Sell yours here" button on the item's product detail page.

You can locate a product detail page using either an ISBN or UPC number. Many products exist in several variations; you want to try to find an **exact match**. For example, if you're selling your "eBay for Dummies" book, and you have the 2nd edition, you may not sell it on the product detail page for the 4th edition.

> ***"What is the most common mistake sellers from eBay are making on Amazon?"***
>
> *I asked an Amazon customer support representative this question. He said the number one mistake is listing a product that is not an exact match to the product detail page.* **eBay** *sellers often think they can find a "close match" and highlight the differences in the "condition notes."*
>
> *For example, say a seller is selling an LP record by The Kinks called "Low Budget." They cannot find a product detail page for the LP, but they have found the CD version. The seller clicks "Sell yours here" and lists the product noting, "this is a vinyl LP – Not the CD" in the condition notes.*
>
> *This is a violation of Amazon's policies. If a buyer purchases this product, and complains, Amazon will side with the buyer every time. Sellers may not use the defense that the buyer should have read the description. The product must match the product detail page exactly. You may add to what is included, such as an accessory, or an artist's signature, but never change the basic product details by means of your condition notes.*

Chapter 8

Managing Your Inventory

Once you have listed some things on Amazon, you'll want to keep an eye on your open listings. You can see your entire inventory by going to your *account management page*. Once there, under the heading "Manage Your Inventory," click the *"View your current inventory"* link to see all your open listings.

You'll see a list of everything you have currently listed on Amazon. You can adjust two things here in bulk. You can adjust quantity and edit your prices. Once you perform either (or both) click *"Save changes"* and your updates will be entered.

NOTE: You will not see the changes reflected immediately. It takes about 15 minutes for edits to show up on this page.

ASIN (Amazon Standard Identification Number)

You will also notice on this page a column that is headed "ASIN / ISBN." This ASIN is the Amazon Standard Identification Number. It's assigned to items to help prevent duplicates in the Amazon catalog. The folks at Amazon are always trying to keep these numbers cleaned up. Sellers have created duplicate product detail pages over the years. There should one per product. At times Amazon will combine these numbers to keep things a bit more tidy in the marketplace.

Another purpose for this number is served when a seller lists an item that does not have any other means of identification. For example, I have posters listed in my account that have none of the other standard identification numbers. So when I created a product detail page, Amazon assigned an ASIN to my product.

SKUs and Your Growing Inventory

You may be familiar with the term "SKU." It stands for Stock Keeping Unit and is a way to keep track of your inventory. As your inventory grows on Amazon, you may find a need for SKUs to keep things organized. Seasoned Amazon sellers suggest starting a SKU system early.

For example, if you have two identical products, in different conditions you cannot sell them under the same SKU.

If you intend on really growing your business on Amazon, learn how to set up a SKU numbering system. Read Amazon's advice on managing SKUs at: http://tinyurl.com/AmazonSKU

> **FAQ - "Can I List Inventory on eBay and Amazon Simultaneously?"**
>
> *Many sellers list their inventory on multiple platforms. The likelihood of selling the same item at the exact same time is small. But if you do, it could cause problems if you don't have enough inventory to go around.*
>
> *If you know your inventory, and immediately cancel any "orphan listings" you may have, you can sell the same inventory on eBay and Amazon.*

Fulfillment by Amazon (FBA)

Amazon has over a decade of experience processing and shipping orders from their warehouses. Not long ago, they decided to share their vast experience with you, the average seller.

How would you like to focus all of your efforts on selling, and have Amazon worry about fulfilling the orders? That is exactly what happens with the Fulfillment by Amazon program. You send your products to Amazon, they store them in their warehouse, customers purchase the products, Amazon then picks, packs and ships the products to your customers. Fulfillment by Amazon is currently available in the United States, United Kingdom, Germany, and Japan.

You do not have to be a large seller to use FBA. There is no minimum on how much you store, or how much you have to sell, to use their services. In fact, you don't even have to sell the products on Amazon. You can use FBA to fulfill orders from other channels, your own website, eBay, or even in-store retail sales.

There are generally speaking, two types of fees associated with FBA. The first is an inventory storage fee. This is determined on a cubic foot per month basis. The fee is initially $.45 per cubic foot per month for the first three quarters, and rises to $.60 per cubic foot on the fourth quarter.

The second fee is the fulfillment fee. This fee varies based on the specifics of the order. There is one chart for Amazon orders and another for non-Amazon orders. In each case the fulfillment fee involves Amazon picking, packing, and shipping the items for you. The prices are quite reasonable and really free up a seller's valuable time to focus on selling and not on fulfillment.

One more good thing about Amazon's FBA program. Amazon will be responsible for all related customer service and order returns sold on Amazon.com. You can find more details about the program at: http://www.amazonservices.com/fulfillment/

Vacation Settings

Do you need some time off? Amazon offers *Vacation Settings* to allow you to decide whether or not shoppers on Amazon.com can view and order your listings. If you would like to *temporarily* remove your open listings from Amazon.com, set your Listing Status to "On Vacation" until you are ready to receive orders again. Once you change the setting, it takes a while for it to go into effect. I'd suggest keeping a close watch for any stray orders until you're sure your vacation settings are active.

To set your Listing Status to "On Vacation," follow these steps in your Seller Account:

1. Click "Store Settings" in the Settings section.

2. In the Vacation Settings section, click the Edit button.

3. Click **Start your Vacation**.

When you set your Listing Status to "On Vacation," all of your listings will be removed from Amazon.com product detail pages and search results within 36 hours. When you are ready to sell again, set your Listing Status to "Active."

To set your Listing Status to "Active," follow these steps in your Seller Account:

1. Click "Store Settings" in the Settings section.

2. In the Vacation Settings section, click the Edit button.

3. Click **End your Vacation**.

When you set your Listing Status to "Active," your listings will begin appearing on Amazon.com product detail pages and in search results within 36 hours.

If you have a Pro Merchant subscription, it will remain active and monthly subscription fees will still be charged if they come due while your Listing Status is set to "On Vacation."

Chapter 9

Making the Sale and Getting Paid

"Amazon.com Payments: Sold, ship now:"

Learn to love those words. When you see an email with that in the subject line it means you have a sale.

One of the most wonderful things about Amazon is when you get that email. The buyer has <u>already paid</u>. There is no chasing them around, no excuses, no time spent trying to collect fees for an unpaid item.

Amazon Payments

Besides what I just mentioned about collecting payment, there is a difference in how you get your money.

First of all, Amazon collects your payments for you. That's a good thing. It makes life easier for you.

Second, your payments are deposited straight into the bank account that you set up when you created your seller account with Amazon. Deposits are made every 14 days. To see your current earnings, you can go to your *account management page* and click the link that says *"view your payments account."* You can see how much you're paying in fees, and how much Amazon is planning to send you and the date of the next automatic transfer.

If you'd like your money sooner, you can click *"Transfer funds now"* and have the funds sent right away.

Chargebacks

A chargeback occurs when a cardholder *contacts their bank* to dispute the charge for an order placed on Amazon. Chargebacks are also known as "charge disputes" and they can be filed for a variety of reasons, ranging from non-receipt of the item ordered to unauthorized use of the credit card.

You may have experience with chargebacks through eBay and PayPal. PayPal offers seller protection that shields qualifying sellers from chargebacks. (And you wondered what all those PayPal fees were for...)

When a customer contacts their credit card company to request a chargeback, the credit card company will contact Amazon to request the transaction details. Then, Amazon will contact you as the seller to request transaction information.

Most of the time, you will be asked for the date the item was shipped, the shipping method used and any tracking information for the shipment. You may also be asked for item information, especially when the customer claims that they received a different item from the one posted on the website. (This is another reason to make sure your item matches the *product detail page exactly*.) You are required to provide all the information outlined in the chargeback notification regarding the disputed transaction. It's a good idea to include any correspondence you may have had with the customer in your response to Amazon.

Amazon's investigator reviews the information provided, creates supporting documentation ("representment") and submits it to the issuing bank on your behalf.

> **FYI:** *To prevent a debit for any dispute, follow good shipping practices. First and foremost, don't change the shipping address provided to you by Amazon as you are liable for any disputes filed for orders you have sent to a different shipping address.*

You can limit your liability by using a shipping method with a tracking number and signature required for high value merchandise. As an eBay seller, you've probably developed a system to keep records of the date the merchandise was shipped, the shipping method used, and any available tracking information. You should keep this information for at least 6 months past the Amazon order date.

Note: Do not ignore a chargeback notification. You must respond within 7 calendar days of the e-mail notification date. If you don't respond, you may be debited for the transaction.

Chapter 10

Packing and Shipping Your Items

This step should be "old hat" for eBayers. If you do well at shipping on eBay, you should be able to handle Amazon shipping. eBay has Amazon beat when it comes to tools to help you ship. You'll have to develop your own process for handling your Amazon orders, but I will share mine to get you started.

Packing Best Practices

It's very important on Amazon to pack professionally. Amazon buyers in general are not charmed by the quaint little old lady packing up items at her kitchen table. They prefer a more professional package. Oblige them. Don't fight it. You won't win.

Use new packing materials, and provide a packing slip. Amazon requires you to include a packing slip in the package. The item condition comments are included on the packing slip. So if you said in the comments for your Simpsons Thermos, "Big dent in Homer's forehead" the buyer cannot say, "Dohh!! I never saw that!"

To print your packing slips, head back to the *account management page* and click the link *"View your orders."* There you can see your current orders and print a packing slip for each one. I've added a sample on the next page:

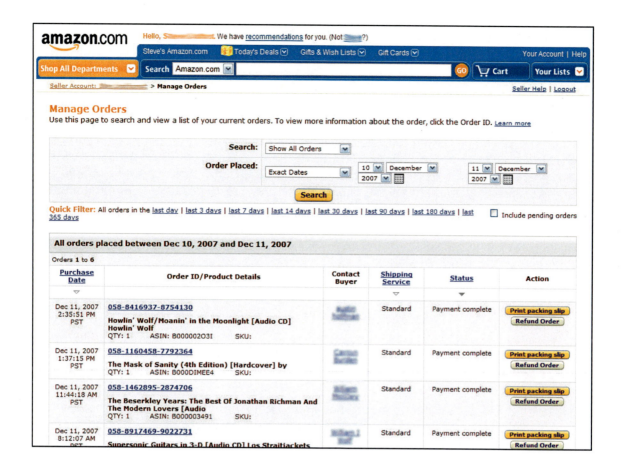

You can also see on this page there is a column titled: "*Contact Buyer*". Each buyer's name is clickable so you can communicate with them through Amazon, much like eBay's "My Messages" feature.

How to Print Shipping Labels for Amazon Orders with PayPal

When I started selling through Amazon, I missed the seamless integration between my eBay seller account and PayPal shipping labels. It's an easy work around. I print my packing slips, and type the addresses into PayPal's Ship Now page. I get the option to ship using Media Mail rate, and I get a trackable, pre-paid label for my package. The payment for the label comes out of my PayPal account.

Visit and bookmark the PayPal Ship Now page at: **http://tinyurl.com/PayPal-Ship-Now**

PayPal MultiOrder Shipping

PayPal's MultiOrder Shipping is a good tool for creating more than one label. Login to your PayPal account. In the left column near the top under the heading "Tools" you'll find the link to MultiOrder Shipping. Click *"File" > "Create New Orders"* and fill out the info.

You can create package presets so you don't have to enter the information for each package. For example, I created a preset I named "Amazon Book" that covers most books I sell. I simply select the preset, and then type in the customer's name. Then I click "Create Another" and it's saved to the queue and I'm on to my next label. Once they are all created, I can print them all out at once. Click Print, then Pay and Continue.

The best part is avoiding the line at the post office. I just walk in and leave my packages in a designated place, and leave. All done!

> **FYI:** *Make sure you have tracking information when shipping your Amazon items. If there is any trouble in the process, you will need documentation.*

Customer Service

Providing great customer service is a sure-fire way to help you stand head and shoulders above the crowd. Selling on eBay has likely imbued you with a quality not seen as often on Amazon. You have developed an ability to pay attention to each and every sale.

Many big Amazon sellers leave out the "personal touch." I'm not talking about putting bags of popcorn in your packages. I'm talking about attention to detail, from accurate product descriptions to shipping promptly using quality packaging. Just good solid customer service. If you get an inquiry from a buyer, answer it promptly and professionally.

Your main goal in retail selling is making money. You will make more money if you pro-vide great customer service. Eventually, you will pick up repeat buyers. It is harder to get loyal repeat buyers on Amazon, but they do exist. In fact, some former eBay sellers have let their regular customers know they've moved to Amazon, and their customers follow.

Dealing with Amazon – Policies You Should Know

Amazon's A-to-z Guarantee

When a customer contacts Amazon about a problem, they may be able to take advantage of Amazon's "A-to-z Guarantee." This is different than a chargeback, since the customer is seeking help from Amazon directly instead of working through their credit card company.

In cases where there is a dispute between buyer and seller, Amazon tends to side with the buyer. There isn't much room for haggling over a matter. Sellers on Amazon agree to abide by the terms of Amazon's A-to-z Guarantee.

Buyers may submit an A-z Guarantee claim in a window between approximately 30 and 90 days from the order date. The seller will receive an email that a claim has been filed. The seller should respond immediately to the claim. Do not ignore an A-z claim, the sooner you respond the better.

There are ways to resolve a claim outlined in detail on Amazon.com. Most are common sense. Failing to respond to an A-z claim though causes you to lose by default. If that happens, Amazon will debit the money from your account and give it back to the buyer.

> *"What is covered under the Amazon.com A-to-z Guarantee?*
>
> 1. *The buyer purchased an item using the Amazon Payments system but never received the item they ordered.*
> 2. *The buyer received the item, but the item was materially different than expected and depicted in the seller's description.*
>
> **When is a product "materially different" than what the seller advertised?**
>
> *If a seller has clearly misrepresented the condition or details of an item in a way that affects its value or utility, it is "materially different" and that seller should be willing to offer a refund or exchange. If the seller does not offer a refund or exchange, the buyer is eligible for our A-to-z Guarantee.*
>
> *Items are considered "materially different" in these circumstances:*
>
> - *Wrong version or edition*
> - *Item condition or details not as described*
> - *Wrong item*
> - *Missing parts or components*
> - *Defective item*
> - *Damaged item*
>
> *When submitting an A-to-z Guarantee claim with the reason "materially different," the buyer will need to select one of the reasons above and provide comments explaining why the item they received is materially different from the item they purchased.*
>
> *Please note that this does not extend to cases where the buyer is simply disappointed with an item. Amazon.com will ultimately determine material difference in accordance with the terms of the A-to-z Guarantee."*

New Seller Reviews

Amazon tries hard to maintain security for buyers and sellers alike. If you are a new seller, there will be a 14-day holding period after you first give them your checking account information. During that time, they will not transfer funds to your checking account. Once your first automatic transfer has taken place, you can disburse funds yourself, every 24 hours if you like.

As a new Amazon seller, you may find great success in the first couple of weeks. If you bust out of the gate with lots of sales, you may have your Amazon payments locked up for a 45-day review. They basically want to see that your customers (read "*their* customer") get what they paid for in a timely manner. Amazon will watch your feedback and refund rate. If you have a high number of refunds or complaints they may terminate your account.

The review period may cause difficulty for new sellers. It means shipping, with all related expenses, and not being reimbursed for a month and a half. Try to be prepared in case your account is put under review. You should be prepared to absorb costs until the hold is over. You *will* get your money after the review. The review is not limited to new sellers. Any time activity in your account changes drastically, you may be flagged, even if you've been selling for some time.

I started out slowly with Amazon sales. In my first month of selling books I had around $500 in sales. The second month I had about the same. In that time, I accumulated a little feedback and no refunds. I never saw the 45 day hold on my account. If I suddenly went from $500 to $5000 in one month, I would likely get Amazon's unwanted attention. Ramp up your sales gradually and you won't set off any red flags causing your funds to be held.

Some sellers complain loudly about the review, but understandably, Amazon wants to protect themselves. If you've sold thousands of dollars worth of goods, how does Amazon know you shipped everything? This is how they tell. Be prepared to pack and ship your items *before* you get your money from Amazon. This is a big difference from the eBay way, but trust me – Amazon is good for the funds, just plan ahead in the beginning.

Velocity Limits

Most sellers won't need this information, but some come out of the gates like gang-busters, so I will briefly discuss "Velocity Limits."

To quote directly from Amazon:

> *"Because Amazon Payments is first and foremost a credit card processing service, we set certain limits on transactions to prevent misuse.*
>
> *How does it work?*
>
> *Selling limits, also known as "velocity limits," are applied to both buyers and sellers. There are limits on both the size of the individual transactions and the total dollar amount processed in a given period. The maximum dollar amount we can process for any individual transaction is $2,475. The amount that a seller can receive in a given time period varies based on our evaluation of the application."*

In other words, you are not going to be allowed to go too fast, too soon. Some sellers (on eBay especially) have listed everything but the kitchen sink, sold it, and then collapsed under the weight of all their orders. Amazon tries to manage that process a little better.

If you would like to learn more about Velocity Limits, visit: **http://tinyurl.com/Velocity-Limits**

Feedback (yes, they have it here too)

eBay sellers are perhaps the world's authorities on feedback comments. Some of eBay's recent changes may have resulted in your purchase of this ebook. Amazon has managed to create a useful feedback system, but without so much emotion.

Generally speaking, feedback is given from buyers to sellers. Sellers can leave feedback for buyers, but there isn't much point to it. As and Amazon seller, you do not have the ability to "block" certain buyers from purchasing from you.

Amazon has a 5-star feedback system whereby a buyer may rate the seller:

- ★ 5 Stars (Excellent)
- ★ 4 Stars (Good)
- ★ 3 Stars (Fair)
- ★ 2 Stars (Poor)
- ★ 1 Star (Awful)

Fives and fours appear as green in your profile. They count as positives. Threes appear as gray, and twos and ones as red. On Amazon the neutral comments (threes) count as negative comments.

There is also a box for comments. Comments will appear in your feedback profile, in much the same way as eBay feedback. You can view your feedback comments from your *manage your account* page.

Optional questions do not count against you, but Amazon does pay attention to them, so mind your Ps and Qs. Amazon is different from eBay in that they do not tinker with search results, based on your feedback. Feedback speaks for itself, and buyers can make their own choice.

Once a buyer leaves feedback for a seller, they have 60 days to change their mind and remove their comment.

Most sellers seem to think Amazon feedback does not carry as much weight as eBay feedback. I agree. But when I'm faced with a choice of products, and all other things are equal, feedback will be a tie-breaker for me. So try to maintain great feedback.

Amazon Phone Support

(Yes, I said *phone,* can you believe that?)

Being able to speak to a human when problems arise is very important. eBay members have complained for years about lack of phone support. Amazon offers phone support.

Amazon's phone support is called the "Click to call" service. You can click "Help" from any page, and you'll see a simple page that offers options such as Express, E-mail, and Phone. Select the "Phone" tab, and click "Call Me." A small box will appear asking for your phone number ***and the time you'd like them to call*** ("Right Now" is an option).

Click the "Submit" button and you'll receive a phone call at the number you specified. It's great! There is support for both buyers and sellers. If you feel you have the wrong one, they will happily transfer you.

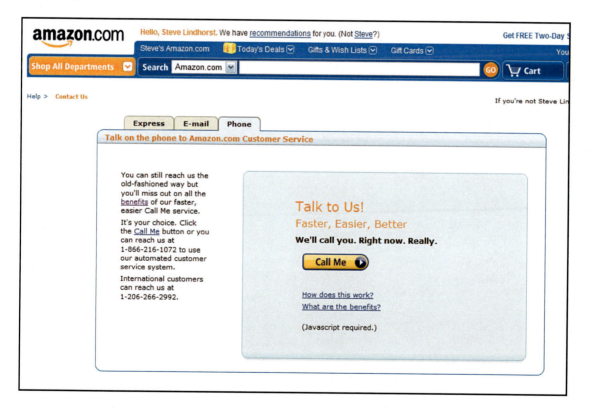

Summary

I hope this guide will help you get your start as a seller on Amazon. As I mentioned earlier, I don't feel this is a replacement for eBay. eBay has its place, and Amazon has its place. Selling on both platforms will make you a wealthier person. You will sell more eggs with two baskets. You also protect yourself against 100% loss – no matter who's at fault.

My advice is to get your seller account set up as soon as possible. Set up your bank account. That way you'll get that 14-day waiting period started, and when you have money coming to you, you likely won't have to wait.

Next, get something to sell. I recommend starting with books. They are easy to list, and I'll bet you already have some sitting around the house. Don't try to make a killing right off the bat. Just list some things. It may take some time to get a sale, but don't give up. Once you have learned the listing process a little better, move to other items.

Try to gradually grow your sales and build good feedback. This may help you avoid the dreaded 45-day review period.

Stay on top of your customer service. That will be your lifeline as your sales grow on Amazon.

Amazon has programs to help you grow as a seller. You should stay abreast of what they have to offer. Just as with eBay, Amazon is a place to sell, learn the rules and abide by them. Learn about the programs and tools they offer, and let them help you grow.

Comparing eBay and Amazon is like comparing apples and oranges. Understand the differences. There really isn't a sense of "community" at Amazon that compares to eBay's community. People are there to buy and sell.

Remember why you are selling things: to get paid. You are paid for your work. You are not paid to socialize, or be happy. You are paid only if you work hard, and sell things.

Resources for Amazon Sellers

Amazon Customer Service Phone Number 1-866-216-1072
International customers dial 1-206-266-2992

Amazon Seller Community.....www.AmazonSellerCommunity.com

Amazon Seller Support.........www.AmazonSellerSupportBlog.com

Sign up for the Steve's free newsletter for selling tips and advice at www.MultichannelSurfer.com.

Blogs That Discuss Selling on Amazon

- www.MultichannelSurfer.com
- www.AmazonStrategies.com
- www.myBlogUtopia.com
- www.AuctionBytes.com
- www.bookthink.com
- www.WeberBooks.com

Sign up for the Steve's free newsletter for selling tips and advice at:

www.MultichannelSurfer.com

Made in the USA
San Bernardino, CA
04 September 2015